ENGLISH FOR ACADEMIC STUDY SERIES

STUDY SKILLS FOR ACADEMIC WRITING

Teacher's Book

John Trzeciak
and S. E. Mackay

PHOENIX
ELT

incorporating
PRENTICE HALL MACMILLAN

New York   London   Toronto   Sydney   Tokyo   Singapore

Property of
EIS Unit
UoD

Other titles in the English for Academic Study series:

MCGOVERN, D., MATTHEWS, M.
and MACKAY, S. E.
Reading

WHITE, R. and MCGOVERN, D.
Writing

The English for Academic Purposes series:

ST JOHN YATES, C.
Agriculture

ST JOHN YATES, C.
Economics

VAUGHAN JAMES, C.
Business Studies

JOHNSON, D. and JOHNSON, C. M.
General Engineering

WALKER, T.
Computer Studies

JAMES, D. V.
Medicine

ST JOHN YATES, C.
Earth Sciences

First published 1994 by
Prentice Hall Europe
Campus 400, Maylands Avenue
Hemel Hempstead
Hertfordshire, HP2 7EZ
A division of
Simon & Schuster International Group

© Prentice Hall Europe 1997

All rights reserved. No reproduction, copy or transmission
of this publication may be made save with written permission
or in accordance with the provisions of the Copyright, Designs
and Patents Act 1988, or under the terms of any licence
permitting limited copying issued by the Copyright Licensing
Agency, 90 Tottenham Court Road, London, W1P 9HE.

Typeset in 11/12 Garamond
by Fakenham Photosetting Limited

Printed and bound in Great Britain by
Redwood Books, Trowbridge, Wiltshire

British Library Cataloguing in Publication Data

A catalogue record for this book is available from the British Library

ISBN 0-13-303728-2

5   4   3
1999   98   97

CONTENTS

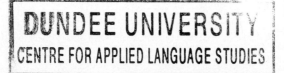

DUNDEE UNIVERSITY
CENTRE FOR APPLIED LANGUAGE STUDIES

INTRODUCTION

AIMS

The material in the Student's Book is designed to explain and give practice in important skills that students require to write an extended academic essay in English. It is aimed principally at overseas students planning to study for a higher degree in a university or college in which English is the main medium of instruction.

While assuming a certain minimum language proficiency ('Intermediate', IELTS band 5/5.5, TOEFEL 490–515) for students starting this book, the material is designed to meet the needs of students who may have little acquaintance with study skills. It is also intended to provide useful revision for those whose background may mean that they already have considerable familiarity with many of the skills covered, having used them in working in their own language.

To write an extended academic essay in English, students will need to be able to:

- extract relevant information from reading sources
- take relevant and adequate notes
- summarise and/or integrate ideas without plagiarism
- produce a coherent, well-organised piece of written work
- lay out work correctly (title and contents pages, bibliography etc.).

It is hoped that by covering the material in this book and completing the tasks of writing extended essays in the last two units, students will acquire sufficient study skills and general language skills to make their period of study in an English-speaking institution of higher education less of an ordeal and more of a pleasure, as well as a success.

There is little overt attention given to the teaching of language in the material. However, considerable care has been taken in selecting texts with suitable metalanguage (i.e. language used to talk about other language) and reinforcing it by repeated examples in the units. It is intended that by working their way through the material, students will acquire metalanguage through gradual familiarisation.

Since there is a large amount of existing published material providing general guidelines on using libraries, and since the specifics of library usage in different English-speaking academic institutions may vary, we have not focused on library skills in the Student's Book.

ORGANISATION OF MATERIAL

In each unit, students should go through the Guide section before the Tasks section; however, it is possible to follow class coverage of selected skills with corresponding tasks. The Guide can be used for self-study by students; teachers will have to evaluate the levels of their students to decide how much attention to give to the Guide in class. For example, many students may be familiar with note-taking skills (in Unit 2), in which case it may be preferable to cover only some of the tasks for revision purposes or to ascertain familiarity with skills.

There are a few instances where short tasks appear in the Guide section. They have been included there because of their importance in supporting a point – their inclusion in the Tasks section would only have disrupted continuity in the Guide. To facilitate teachers' use of the material, these short tasks are listed here:

UNIT	SKILL	PAGE
1	Anticipating content by title	5
2	Identifying main purpose and functions of text from the introduction	21
	Note-taking	22
	Summarising	27
3	Examples of reporting verbs	62
	Dividing a text into paragraphs (2 tasks)	62

FEATURES OF MATERIAL

CONTENT

There is a small element of progression in the language difficulty of the extracts chosen from other sources, as well as in the main text, from Units 1 to 4. There is also a certain amount of allowance for different language levels in some of the tasks. In the case of tasks which offer alternatives (see, for example, Unit 1, Task 7; Unit 2, Task 10; or Unit 3, Task 3), it can always be assumed that the first text/task is linguistically and intellectually the less/least demanding while the second (or last) is the more/most demanding.

The intellectual difficulty is related to the degree of accessibility of material to non-specialists. In the case of those tasks where a thorough reading of the text is required, it is hoped that the texts chosen will prove interesting and accessible to most students. In those tasks where alternative texts are offered, a greater degree of interest and accessibility is evident in the first text. It should be noted, however, that some texts are not intended to be read thoroughly for content; they are meant to focus the students' attention on language which reflects the features being examined (such as the features of introductions and conclusions in Unit 3, Tasks 7 and 8).

Every effort has been made to cover as wide a range of topics as possible and to include texts that are interesting and of durable value. To a small extent, tasks which offer a choice of texts also offer the possibility of meeting students' subject needs.

In most cases, authentic academic texts have been used. Where newspaper articles have been included, it is because it was felt that the value of their short length and accessibility of content outweighed the disadvantage of the loss of features such as development of ideas and longer paragraphs. Texts written in 'journalese' have been largely excluded.

FOCUS ON PLAGIARISM

Considerable emphasis has been placed on tackling the problem of plagiarism. While it might be argued that, at certain stages of acquiring a foreign language, copying as a way of learning does no harm, the undesirability of this practice in higher academic study persuades us to discourage it under any circumstances. Moreover, the practice of paraphrasing, though difficult to acquire for some, is, at the language level of students working with this book, a highly useful way of improving their flexibility and proficiency in English usage.

Questions as to what exactly constitutes plagiarism at the level of both language and ideas may sometimes be open to debate and disagreement. This issue may be raised by some of the tasks in Unit 2, tasks which are designed to promote discussion and polemic in class. It is not our intention to 'sweep under the carpet' questions of what exactly constitutes plagiarism; however, we do not see it as useful to lay down precise guidelines in the Student's Book as to what is an unacceptable level of similarity in wording or ideas. If students themselves perceive a need for greater precision, teachers are referred to the discussion of plagiarism in the notes on Unit 2 in this book, entitled 'A brief digression on plagiarism'.

INCORPORATING AND ACKNOWLEDGING SOURCE MATERIAL

A deliberate distinction is made in Unit 2 between tasks designed to focus on paraphrasing for a summary (Tasks 4–6), where summarising is seen as an objective in itself, and tasks focusing on acceptable incorporation of another's writing. The latter may involve paraphrase or quotation and always demand acknowledgement (Unit 2, Task 10, as well as Tasks 1, 2 and 3 in Unit 3). While the importance of acknowledgement should be stressed, it is hoped that there are sufficient examples in the material to encourage students to adopt the practice in their own writing without too much repeated insistence on the part of the teacher. Acceptable ways of incorporating source material are gradually introduced in Units 2 and 3, starting with the work on note-taking and summarising, which are seen as useful practices in safeguarding against tendencies to plagiarise.

IMPORTANCE OF THE FINAL TASK

The *final* task in the material – writing an extended essay in a student's own subject area – should be stressed at the outset to allow students to start thinking about the subject of their essay and, if they have access to a library, even begin to *collect references when they have completed the second unit.* The tasks in Units 1–4 allow students to practise the skills necessary to produce a satisfactory extended essay when they have finished Unit 4.

If students have access to published material in their own area and are able to do the extended writing tasks, it is important to stress that they should choose a subject that is within their grasp and not 'bite off more than they can chew'. A drawback of exposing students to published material in their own subject is that they sometimes feel they have to emulate what they read in terms of language and sophistication of thought. This can increase the temptation to plagiarise. It is very important to dissuade students from this habit before they embark on a main course, even if it is initially achieved at some cost in quality of language and content. From the outset, it may be advisable to stress less preoccupation with linguistic perfection and more with actually thinking through material so that it is expressed in the student's own words.

A distinction is made between the shorter task in Unit 4, which stresses presentation and skills such as writing references and quotations, and the extended writing task in Unit 5. In the task in Unit 5, students are expected to have mastered the above skills. It is important to ensure that they have command of reference skills and do not regard them as a triviality. If they can master these skills when working on the essay at the end of Unit 4, they can be free to focus more on content in the final writing task.

The last units are intentionally shorter than previous ones to allow time to concentrate on the extended writing tasks. For these, the teacher will have a greater supervisory role.

DEVELOPMENT AND USAGE OF THE MATERIALS

Some of the tasks in this book focus on areas that have not been given great attention in previous published study skills material. Some of the texts are intended to provide an intellectual challenge which is sometimes underplayed in EAP work. Most of the material has been trialled successfully on the Pre-sessional Course at the Centre for Applied Language Studies at the University of Reading. It was designed to be covered in a period of 11–12 weeks, with eight hours in the classroom per week being devoted to the skills covered, allowing reasonable time for students to do the extended writing tasks at the end (3–4 weeks). Clearly, it is difficult to be prescriptive in recommending a time-scale for using the book, since this will depend on factors such as students' language level, familiarity with English-speaking academic conventions and access to a library.

UNIT 1

SURVEYING MATERIAL

AIMS

This unit aims to provide students with a basis for surveying and selecting appropriate materials. That is, students should be able to evaluate the *usefulness* of a particular article or book.

The following activities will be covered in this unit:

- surveying material (a book or article)
- recording essential information.

SURVEYING MATERIAL

Many weaker students may have difficulty in assessing the usefulness of a particular book; that is how relevant the content is to their work, whether it is outdated, whether it is a key text etc. Also, many students feel the need to read a particular book from cover to cover (even if sections are not relevant) and/or they do not know how to select possible sections suitable for sources of information. Thus, they may select an outdated or unsuitable book/article, or dismiss a book/article because they do not immediately find a direct reference to the topic they are interested in. It is hoped that the tasks in this section will develop skills that prevent them from wasting time in these ways.

For many students, features such as title and contents page will be very familiar and this unit can be covered very rapidly. Care should be taken not to appear patronising in introducing features of a book to those who may be familiar with them from their own language.

For students who may have trouble with the material, it is worth checking at the outset whether they know where the following are found in a book:

- author's name
- sub-title
- publisher
- date of publication
- place of publication.

The 'Surveying' material contains tasks on the following:

- prediction questions on book titles
- use of the contents page
- use of the index
- looking at blurbs
- surveying a text
- looking at introductions
- looking at the printing history of a book.

TASK 2: ANSWERS

(a) Part 5

(b) Part 4

(c) Part 2

(d) Part 6

(e) Part 1

(f) Part 3

TASK 3: ANSWERS

(a) Chapter 2.2

(b) Chapter 4.1

(c) Chapter 6.3

(d) Chapter 1.2

(e) Chapter 3.4

(f) Chapter 5.1

TASK 4: ANSWERS

(a) 140–1

(b) 21

(c) 148–9, 152–5

(d) 56–8

TASK 6: ANSWERS

1. (a) Its seeds consist of up to one-third vegetable oil.
   (b) It will grow in a wide variety of soils.
   (c) It is a short-season crop, well-suited to the climatic conditions in Britain.

2. (a) World pressure is resulting in the reduction of whale oil for commercial uses; therefore a replacement is needed.
   (b) It is green and smelly.

(c) Meadowfoam can be easily integrated with the rape-seed harvest.

(d) Petroselenic acid contained in the seeds could be split to produce lauric acid, which is at present extracted from palm kernel and coconut.

Task 7: Answers

1. (c)   2. (c)

Task 8

Note that, when deciding which date to use, reprints are usually ignored; it is most common to use the date of the latest edition.

UNIT

2 NOTE-TAKING AND SUMMARISING SKILLS

AIMS

The aims of this unit are as follows:

- to give practice in extracting main/relevant/supporting ideas from a text or article
- to ensure that students can take useful notes
- to ensure that students are able to summarise ideas without 'lifting' sections of a text verbatim.

Although most students will have had practice in note-taking, many may still be unable to recognise main ideas in a text. Students often have a tendency to make notes on everything, rather than being selective. A further problem is an inability to summarise clearly in their own words. A tendency to plagiarise in producing a piece of extended writing can be a major problem in students' work. This perhaps stems from the fact that many students have a different academic background from that of an English-speaking country, perhaps from a lack of confidence in their own command of English and/or from an inability to extract relevant information from a text. It is important to emphasise that plagiarism is unacceptable and can readily be detected. This unit is therefore primarily concerned with developing good note-taking skills and students' confidence in their own ability to summarise/report ideas without resorting to copying from source material.

As well as practising note-taking and summary-writing, this unit also aims to encourage students to be selective in extracting from a text only the information that is relevant to the topic they are writing on.

At this stage, it is of the utmost importance to stress that students must use their own words in academic work (apart from, of course, quotations). Even students of a high language level often have difficulty in extracting and summarising information. For this reason, all students should benefit from the material in this unit. With good students the emphasis should be on summarising skills rather than note-taking, although you might like to use one of the note-taking tasks (Tasks 1–3) to check their note-taking skills.

The texts used in this unit are of a general academic nature. Nevertheless, students may show resistance to some of the content. To some extent, however, there is room for choice on the basis of students' subject orientation rather than language ability.

Note-taking

This section is meant to provide examples of different styles only; they are not intended to be rigidly prescriptive. Students may have developed their own style of note-taking which, even if not ultra-economical, serves their purposes adequately. 'Mind-mapping' can be suggested as a useful exercise for EFL learners at this stage in their studies – it can help not only to avoid plagiarism but also to practise expressing ideas in English with a minimum of information. For many students, this section will be purely for quick revision and is not to be dwelt on. For some, it may be necessary to teach note-taking from scratch – students may think that copying 'relevant' chunks of text is enough. On the other hand, those who are well acquainted with techniques may still have considerable trouble isolating main ideas.

Summarising

Both the note-taking (previous section) and summarising work are intended to help protect students from the temptation of plagiarising. There is both cognitive and linguistic progression in the way the summarising material has been arranged. Start with a discussion of the alternative brief summaries in the short task in the Guide section ('Salaries rise in line with fees'), ensuring that students cover the bottom half of page 28. You can then move on to the summarising work in the Tasks section.

The tasks that follow involve choosing satisfactory summaries from a range of alternatives. Task 5 focuses on summarising a whole text (global summarising), while Task 6 involves looking at summaries of only part of the information in a text (selective summarising). These are intended as a focus for class discussion before students go on to do the other summarising tasks. Tasks 7 and 8 should be done by students individually, while Task 9 involves group work.

The alternative summaries in Tasks 5 and 6 are designed to focus students' attention on the skills of paraphrasing and summarising. It should become apparent to students that acquiring these skills can prevent the tendency to plagiarise. However, detailed focus on what actually constitutes plagiarism is left to the task at the end of the unit (Task 10). In case students become confused, *it is important to point out* that the alternatives which follow the text in Task 10 are *not* summaries but examples of acceptable and unacceptable ways of incorporating source material into a student's writing. This section is intended to serve as a direct bridge to the more detailed work on referencing and quotations in Unit 3.

Note: Do not forget that you do not have to cover all the tasks. Select those which would most benefit your class, taking into consideration both the language level and subject orientation of your students.

Jigsaw summarising is the only activity which is specifically designed for small group work. But, if you so wish, all the other tasks could also be tackled in pairs/ small groups.

Brief description of individual task aims

There is an extra task on note-taking in Appendix 2 at the end of this Teacher's Book (p. 38). This gives general help on note-taking. Include this task at the stage where it would be most helpful to your students, especially if they run into difficulties with note-taking.

TASKS 1 AND 2

These short tasks are designed to test a basic grasp of note-taking.

TASK 3

The discussion after Task 2 is intended to emphasise the desirability of basing a summary on notes (option (e)). Task 3 is designed to show how information from notes can be transferred to a brief summary.

TASK 4: SUMMARISING SHORT PASSAGES IN ONE OR TWO SENTENCES

This task is designed to encourage students to select main points only and should be done quickly. You might like to discuss briefly the role of supporting information in the texts.

TASKS 5 AND 6: CHOOSING SATISFACTORY GLOBAL AND SELECTIVE SUMMARIES

These tasks focus on *global* summarising and *selective* summarising. While it has not been possible to provide a wider range of texts covering several major fields, the first article in each task, 'Fire stones support catastrophe theory' and 'Japan paves way for big foreign influx' is of a sufficiently general nature to be accessible intellectually to most students.

Note that in the summary examples, reference to the source is always made. This is done to make students aware of the importance of acknowledgement – it is not necessary at this stage to go into details. These are focused on in Task 10 (as well as Unit 3, Tasks 1 and 2). The question of acknowledging paraphrased writing is discussed in the section entitled 'A brief digression on plagiarism' on page 19 in this book.

TASKS 7 AND 8: GLOBAL AND SELECTIVE NOTE-TAKING AND RECONSTITUTION

These are designed to combine note-taking and summarising practice. Task 8 is guided, in that students are told what information to look for.

TASK 9: JIGSAW SUMMARISING

What do a Vietnamese pheasant, an Iraqi lizard, hundreds of Indonesian butterflies and a tiny beetle in an Essex compost heap have in common? They are all species that are 'new to science', that is, first scientifically described in the past few years. The work of describing new species, and revising the names of existing species, is done by taxonomists, an unfashionable and dwindling group of scientists most of whom work in the developed world. Britain used to be a major contributor but as government funding here has been reduced, most of it now takes place in Europe, America and Japan, where governments still support taxonomic study.

The science of taxonomy was started in the late eighteenth century by Swedish biologist Carl Linnaeus. With a small number of similarly minded scientists he pioneered a standard system, using two Latin names denoting 'genus' and 'species', that is still in use today. Every species of plant or animal 'known to science' has a two-part Latin name, such as *Homo sapiens*, the Latin name for the human species. A species is an actually or potentially successful breeding population. The importance of the taxonomists' work, as the basis of modern biology, cannot be overestimated. Without an animal or plant having a universally agreed identity, no two scientists can be sure they are looking at the same species.

Scientific nomenclature is based on extensive, preserved collections with which newly found specimens can be compared. These museum collections, especially the tropical ones, are mostly in Western Europe; in Britain, France, Germany and the Netherlands. Many European naturalists travelled widely in the tropics, collected large numbers of specimens, and brought them back to their own national collections. Our own Natural History Museum is one of the most important. It houses hundreds of thousands of specimens of unique taxonomic value from birds' eggs to tarantulas and from lemmings to bees.

In Britain the discovery of a species 'new to science' is a rare event; a cause for celebration among naturalists. This is why the tiny species of 'feather-wing beetle' from Essex is of interest. Each year perhaps three small moths (*Microlepidoptera*) and a handful of other insects are described from Britain, but for tropical countries, like Indonesia or Papua New Guinea, the task of collecting and naming the myriad species is not far advanced. It is an urgent task. A recent expedition to the island of Sulewesi produced several hundred new moths and butterflies alone. There are very few countries outside northern Europe where even a rudimentary species list for the main groups of insects could be prepared. Even the much less diverse birds, amphibians and reptiles are not fully known. Both the Vietnamese pheasant and the Iraqi lizard were 'new to science'; how many more animals large and small await first sighting in the deserts of the Middle East or the forests of Vietnam?

(Adapted from J. E. Milner, 'Why it is absolutely essential to carry on naming names', *The Independent*, 1.8.88.)

Here students work in small groups. Each group is to extract the main idea from a section of the text below and summarise it in one sentence. The groups should then re-form so that in each new group there is one member for each section of the text. The summarised main ideas should then be arranged and/or rewritten to form a coherent piece of discourse. The fact that this task is done as a jigsaw exercise means that the students will need to have summarised each section clearly in order for the whole to make sense. It should also draw attention to factors such as the necessity for correct cohesion, reference, grammar etc.

Photocopy the text and cut it into four. Be sure to cut off the text source. Divide the class into four groups, each having a section of the text to summarise in one sentence. The class should then regroup so that there is one person from each original group in each new group. These final groups then arrange the summaries into a coherent order, checking for any necessary changes in cohesion, grammar etc.

TASK 10: AVOIDING PLAGIARISM

It is worth pointing out to students that these are not summaries but examples of acceptable and unacceptable incorporations of source material. It should also be stressed that incorporating source material in a satisfactory way is not simply a question of rewording the original. Students should be made aware of the most effective *process* of working – taking notes but copying only where material is felt suitable for quotation.

TASK 11: SUMMARISING AN ARTICLE

This task is intended both to practise and check the skills covered so far and is intended as an alternative or additional task to the text in Task 6 above. The inclusion of a justification for their choice of article is aimed at encouraging students to evaluate the appropriacy of their choice and to raise awareness in selecting suitable materials.

If students have access to published material, they should be encouraged to do this task even if they are not yet very familiar with their future subject of study.

TASK 1: ANSWERS

Romantic landscape photography – many styles:

1. Pastoral (e.g. G. Davies – followed painterly influences)

    Features:
    (a) softness:
        (i)   soft-focused and diffused lenses
        (ii)   shallow focus
        (iii) soft-printing
        (iv)   fast film (graininess).

(b) subject matter:
    (i)   comfortable
    (ii) familiar
    (iii) rural.

(c) contrived & dominated by technique.

2. Drama and grandeur

Examples:
(a) Ansel Adams
    (i) visualised pictures clearly
    (ii) exploited dramatic potential by:
      • timing
      • composition.

(b) Modern magazine photography

Extreme presentation of drama in:
(i)   subjects e.g. mountains & deserts;
(ii) lighting e.g. low sun, dusk & dawn;
(iii) design e.g. extreme focal length & high sky-to-land ratios.

NB: Apparent impression of spontaneity false.

TASK 2: ANSWERS

(1) animals
(2) dolomite (magnesium calcium carbonate) carnallite (magnesium calcium chloride)
(3) land
(4) element
(5) by plants
(6) intake
(7) body
(8) functions
(9) needed for building proteins
(10) can be welded
(11) light
(12) 500,000 tons
(13) sulphur
(14) frames

TASK 3: ANSWERS

Notes

(1) Asian cities
(2) hand-pushed carts
(3) NMVs
(4) cars
(5) cheap, quick, convenient
(6) support/actively encourage
(7) people cycling to work

Summary

(1) bicycles, rickshaws and hand-
    pushed carts
(2) environment

(3) government policy
(4) extensive cycle paths
(5) be offered subsidies.

TASK 4: ANSWERS

(a) The effect of disasters is far worse in poor areas of the world than in rich areas.

(b) The impoverishment of British flora and fauna in comparison to the diversity found in other climates is a result of the last Ice Age.

TASK 5: ANSWERS

1.

Summary	Comment
3 and 6	Clearly unsatisfactory! 3 refers to a nuclear catastrophe and is very incomplete; 6 gives personal opinion twice – 'I think ...' and last sentence.
4	Unsatisfactory – too wordy, redundant information: no mention of tree-ring data research.
5	May be acceptable as a *brief* summary but does not mention tree-ring data research at all.
1	Fails to give emphasis to research on stones as *main* topic of original article; otherwise satisfactory.
2	The most satisfactory – complete; effective paraphrase.

There may be some disagreement about which of the above is the most satisfactory. Any discussion about which is the best summary can be continued with the question and checklist that follow the alternative summaries. Students should be encouraged to see the most successful approach to summary-writing as one that involves working from notes on the original text rather than simply a 'copy – delete' strategy, which encourages plagiarism or, at best, results in work that is partially modified and may not be fully understood by the student.

CHARACTERISTICS OF AN EFFECTIVE SUMMARY: ANSWERS

(a) Not necessarily – it may sometimes be convenient to have a different order.

(b) No.

(c) Yes, very likely.

(d) No – a common fault.

(e) No – students may sometimes think it is desirable to include personal opinion, as in 6 above.

(f) Not necessarily – expressing an idea more concisely may require greater sophistication of vocabulary.

(g) Yes.

IMPORTANT STEPS IN WRITING AN EFFECTIVE SUMMARY: ANSWERS

All the steps mentioned may be desirable or useful, except (b). Steps (c) and (e) may require some explanation.

2.

Summary	Comment
1 and 2	Both acceptable, though clearly 1 is more detailed.
3	First statement is inaccurate.
4	Accurate but too brief and general.
5	Inaccurate – very loosely linked to the source text.
6	Inaccurate – the writer does not suggest that biopolitics 'is likely to gain increasing acceptance' or that 'changes in the enviroment and in human behaviour can be bought about through political processes'. The last statement is also untrue.
7	Grossly inaccurate, with extraneous information and a concluding statement that has no basis in the source text.

TASK 6: ANSWERS

1.

Summary	Comment
1	First two sentences are irrelevant – summary is meant to focus on scientists, not students; rest is incomplete – no mention of poor working conditions and prospects.
2	Wrong emphasis – Tonegawa's criticism is not the main point.
3	Too close to original – follows vocabulary and sentence patterns of original (lacking conciseness as a result).
4	Acceptable.

2.

Summary	Comment
1	Brief but accurate
2	Long-winded, partly irrelevant and expressing an opinion (in the last sentence) which is not in the text. Use of term 'tropical rain forests' is wrong (see below).
3	Accurate except for use of term 'tropical *rain* forest', suggesting that this covers all types of forest in the tropics. The text divides tropical forests into dry and moist. The latter *includes* rain forests but is not synonymous.
4	First paragraph is not wholly relevant to topic; third paragraph contains an excess of information and a specious comparison in the last sentence.
5	The most satisfactory summary of the information required – accurate, with a suitable amount of selected detail.

TASK 9: ANSWERS

The paragraph order of the original text is as follows:

1. What do a Vietnamese pheasant ...
2. The science of taxonomy ...
3. Scientific nomenclature ...
4. In Britain ...

TASK 10: ANSWERS

Before tackling this task, teachers are recommended to read the section which follows at the end of this unit, entitled 'A brief digression on plagiarism'.

1.

Extract	Comment
1	Copied almost verbatim, so clearly unacceptable.
2	Acceptable, probably written from notes on the original.
3	Unacceptable – copied with minor modifications. This is still plagiarism.
4	Unacceptable – copied, except for first sentence, which names the source. Some students may think that this is perfectly legitimate.
5	Acceptable – acknowledged quotation.

	6	Unacceptable and revealing a common disguise tactic – one or two original sentences from the student with several basic errors, followed by long pieces of faultless, sophisticated prose! Stress that this is easy to recognise. Be sure to correct the errors in first sentence.
	7	Acceptable – expressed in the student's own words and acknowledged because it is felt the original writer merits acknowledging.
	8	Also acceptable as an alternative way of acknowledging source material.

2.	Extract	Comment
	1	Verbatim copying – clearly unacceptable.
	2	Unacceptable – as in 6 in Task 10, part 1 above. (Make sure you correct the first two sentences and the final one.)
	3	Also a direct copy without acknowledgement. The final two sentences may suggest that the student has a grasp of the content but, clearly, that makes it no more acceptable.
	4	Acceptable. Though the ideas are those of the original, they have been thought through *and re-expressed* in the student's own words.
	5	Unacceptable. Changing a few words (commonly at the beginning or end) does not alter the fact that this is, in essence, lifted from the original.
	6	Acceptable because what is taken from the original is in quotation marks and the source is acknowledged.
	7	Also acceptable. The original writer's point is made with acknowledgement to the writer and not copied.
	8	Unacceptable – acknowledged, then copied – as in Task 10, part 1 above.

A BRIEF DIGRESSION ON PLAGIARISM

In discussing the extracts in Task 10, the point may be made by students or teachers that plagiarism can involve not simply copying from a source but stealing someone else's *ideas* and re-expressing them in one's own words without acknowledgement. After all, if one paraphrases source material successfully, as in the summary tasks, can one leave what one has written unacknowledged?

This should be discouraged; but it may sometimes be difficult to draw the line between what constitutes stealing *original* ideas and re-expressing those which are really common domain. In the first text in Task 10, on 'Vitamins', all the information could fairly comfortably be considered to be commonly known – the offence is more one of using the original author's *words* without acknowledgement in extracts 1, 3, 4 and 6. However, it is sometimes better to be on the safe side – hence, the acknowledgement of paraphrased incorporations (as opposed to quotations) in extracts 7 and 8. This makes the unacknowledged paraphrase in 2 slightly suspect.

In the second text used in Task 10, the observations made by the writer are less obviously common knowledge, even among economists – which might make the example of unacknowledged paraphrase in 4 a little suspect! Other considerations may enter into play here – namely, how specialist the intended readership of a piece of writing is in a specialist journal: acknowledgement of information that is commonly known in the field may be far less imperative for a post-doctoral researcher than for a student doing an essay on an M.A. or M.Sc. course.

With respect to plagiarising words, a predictable doubt that may be voiced by some students is: 'How many words in succession from the original would be considered plagiarism?' The 'gut feeling' response to this is that asking the question is already indicative of a wrong attitude. For the purposes of the material in this book, and probably as a general principle too, it is better to appeal to common sense than to inculcate rules. Of course, a piece of writing may end up with an instance of five consecutive words in the same continuous sequence as in a source text. It is when there are repeated instances of this and/or similar sentence patterns to the original that work should be rejected.

As mentioned in the introduction to this book, the above comments are intended to be of assistance if doubts are raised. The deeper one goes into the issue of plagiarism, the more complex it reveals itself to be. While appreciating that discussion at a more superficial level may fail to produce clear-cut solutions because an underlying complexity exists, we trust that it is possible to appeal to teachers' reasonable judgement both in dealing with the material in this unit and evaluating students' writing in the essay tasks in Units 4 and 5.

UNIT 3

WRITING SKILLS

AIMS

The first aim of this unit is to ensure that students are acquainted with different ways of making reference to source materials and to encourage selectivity in their choice of reference for inclusion in their work.

The unit also aims at developing/revising awareness of the separate parts of an essay or paper (introduction, body, conclusion) and (particularly in the case of weaker students) ensuring that students are aware of the generally accepted conventions governing the structure of a paragraph in written English.

The final tasks in this unit are intended to give students practice both in selecting information to include in an essay and in synthesising this information.

Depending on the abilities of your students, the activities could be conducted in groups or individually.

REPORTING, REFERENCES AND QUOTATIONS

Students need practice in incorporating references and quotations into their work. It is important to discuss how a reporting verb or introductory phrase affects the representation of the information and the author's attitude to it (e.g. *claims* versus *has shown*). Many students are unaware of this and misinterpret the use of these phrases or regard them as interchangeable. Encourage your students to build their own collections of verbs/phrases from their extensive reading, making sure they record a comment on their use (e.g. *neutral, favourable, unfavourable, expresses interest*).

Tasks 1 and 2 go a stage further in drawing attention to acceptable ways of incorporating source material. Students should have had 'initial exposure' at the end of Unit 2 in Task 10 on avoiding plagiarism.

Note that the Guide section contains a task on identifying reporting verbs.

DIVIDING A TEXT INTO PARAGRAPHS

There are sometimes cultural or genre differences as regards what constitutes a paragraph. It is therefore worthwhile spending time on a short discussion of this, as even better students may be unaware of these differences or find it difficult to accept that differences do exist.

The issue of how frequently the 'topic sentence' concept is employed by English native-speaker writers is one that is more likely to arise in discussion among teachers than students. The justification for recommending its use in students' writing is its usefulness as a principle of organisation. Many students may have no concept at all of paragraphing in English. For others, language weakness may make their writing difficult to follow even if they have a sense of organisation. In both cases, encouraging the use of topic sentences can help to mitigate problems.

In the tasks which involve arranging an unparagraphed or jumbled text, students should justify their reasons for dividing the text (Task 5) and for arranging the text as they do (Task 6). If students seem particularly weak in Task 5, tell them to aim for six paragraphs. If students say that they have already done a jumbled text task, point out that Task 9 in Unit 2 laid stress on summarising skills, whereas Task 6 in this unit is intended to concentrate more closely on aspects of cohesion and coherence.

Note that the Guide section contains two tasks on division of paragraphs. The long text on speech differences between the sexes could be exploited beyond the instruction given in the Student's Book, as follows. Tell the students that, as an example of how effective paragraph division can make a text *reader-friendly*, they will read a 500-word text on socio-linguistics, a subject which is probably new to most of them, in half a minute. But first some concepts or ideas can be discussed under the following headings:

1. Different languages spoken by men and women in a community
2. Physically caused differences between sexes
3. Pronunciation differences
4. Social causes of differences
5. Vocabulary and grammar differences

After discussion, students can survey-read the text in at least half a minute. You can move from this to Tasks 5 and 6 in the Tasks section.

WRITING INTRODUCTIONS AND CONCLUSIONS

Students often have trouble knowing exactly what to put into an introduction or a conclusion. Common faults include omitting background and objectives in an introduction, or regarding a conclusion as synonymous with a summary. In the conventions of some cultures, a summary of the whole work appears to be an obligatory part of the conclusion. The tasks in this section are designed to draw attention to main features. Students should not be put off by the unfamiliar content of the texts but rather be made to focus on language they recognise as being characteristic of these features, (i.e. metalanguage). It is recommended that all students who were able to come to grips with the tasks in Unit 2 and the first part of this unit attempt Tasks 7–9.

Before doing Tasks 7 and 8, it may be worth asking students, with books closed to restate what they think are important characteristics of introductions and conclusions. They could also be asked to try to identify the subject areas of the extracts *without* attempting to understand the content.

A further task (Task 10) involves looking at the main body of an essay on 'International migration' and choosing a suitable introduction and conclusion for it. This is a difficult exercise which goes beyond examining the material in the light of the criteria considered in Tasks 7 and 8. It should be attempted *only* with a good class – it may confuse weak students. (Task 10 does serve to some extent as a bridge to the additional task in Unit 5, which also considers style.)

SYNTHESISING FROM MORE THAN ONE SOURCE

Synthesising ideas from different sources is often difficult for students. The texts in Task 11 are designed to give them some exposure to the mechanics and language involved. The examples used in the task exemplify common forms of synthesis. It may be worth telling students that many variations exist. Weaker students should then attempt Task 12. This task is designed to be more teacher-led in order to assist students in recognising and adopting an appropriate course of action in synthesising ideas. It may therefore be best to have them working in groups where they have the opportunity to discuss their actions as they progress through the task. The first and final drafts may be done individually or may be produced by the whole group. Suggest that students use columns to list main points. Task 13 may be done with less help from the teacher.

TASK 1: ANSWERS

Extract 3 is unacceptable – full details of reference should go in footnote or references.

TASK 2: ANSWERS

Extracts 1, 3 and 4 exemplify acceptable references and quotations. Note the quotation within the quotation in 1. Extract 2 gives too may details of the sources. The numbers in extract 4 refer to a bibliography – an acceptable form in science subjects.

TASK 3: ANSWERS

1. 'It must be borne in mind ...' (Boas, 1911) can be inserted in its entirety after 'without counting.'
   It could also be inserted in the following form in the same place: As Boas (1911) states, 'counting does not become necessary ...'.

2. (a) Insert after 'far from accurate.' However, note that length of quotation necessitates indentation as a separate paragraph with no quotation marks. This should be preceded by a phrase such as 'As Short (1989) has observed, ...'.

3. (a) Straight insertion of complete sentence after 'came to a conclusion.' in the third paragraph also necessitates indentation due to length. The sentence could be integrated in part into the text, thus:

   ... came to a conclusion. He showed that 'according to the molecular-kinetic theory of heat, bodies of microscopically-visible size suspended in a liquid will perform movements of such magnitude that they can be easily observed in a microscope, on account of the molecular motions of heat' (Einstein, 1926). Einstein's findings ...

3(a) may be difficult for non-science students, though an understanding of the first paragraph should enable them to insert the quotation in the correct place in the third.

TASK 4: ANSWERS

(a) (i) Destruction is very serious – worse than ever ('without precedent'); irreplaceable sites are damaged daily.
    (ii) Most common cause of damage is building of large public works such as dams or highways.

(b) (i) Similarity – both are motivated by inner compulsion.
    (ii) Dissimilarity – society does not hold artists accountable for their actions, whereas scientists are expected to produce tangible results.

TASK 5: ANSWERS

The organisation of paragraphs as they appeared in the original was as follows:

1. The global steel industry ...
2. While developing countries ...
3. Even though world production ...
4. International trade ...

Task 6: Answers

The order of paragraphs as they appear in the original is as follows:

1. An unprecedented £25,000 …
2. The research stems from …
3. Dr. Stradling argues that …
4. Following the success of …
5. The period chosen …
6. Grove …
7. Among the papers …

Task 7: Answers

Feature 1. Introduction 1, first paragraph, first sentence.
Introduction 2, first paragraph, first two sentences.
Introduction 3, first paragraph, first sentence.
Introduction 4, first paragraph, first two sentences.

Feature 2. Introduction 1, first and second paragraphs.
Introduction 2, first paragraph.
Introduction 4, first sentence, referring to footnote.

Feature 3. Introduction 1, first paragraph, last sentence.
Introduction 2, first paragraph, third sentence.

Feature 4. Introduction 1, second paragraph, first and fourth sentences.
Introduction 2, first paragraph, second sentence.
Introduction 3, first paragraph, second sentence.
Introduction 4, third paragraph.

Feature 5. Introduction 3, last sentence '… is beyond the scope of …'.
Stating limitations seems to be more common in conclusions (see Task 8 below) but is not infrequent in introductions.

Feature 6. Introduction 1, second paragraph.
Introduction 2, third paragraph.
Introduction 3, third paragraph.
Introduction 4, third and fourth paragraphs.

Feature 7. Introduction 2, first paragraph.
Where differing viewpoints exist, as in Introduction 2, they will normally be mentioned in an introduction.

Feature 8. Introduction 2, second paragraph, 'I think it likely …'.

Feature 9. This is much more likely to come in a conclusion, if at all.

Feature 10. A definition could appear in an introduction but is probably equally likely in the main body.

It is worth noting that the use of the first person in presenting *views* in academic writing should be undertaken with some caution, particularly in scientific papers where the legitimacy of such use may be confined to speculations and hypotheses at the frontiers of pioneering research.

However, this does not preclude the use of the first person in stating intentions, describing personal experience or reporting an experiment, as in introduction 1, second paragraph: 'In this paper we report on an investigation …'. It can be a useful exercise to ask students to identify such uses of the first person in texts – see, for example, Unit 1, Task 7, second text, fourth paragraph: 'I argue that …'; Unit 3, Task 4, text (b).

While the use of the first person in general may be greater than is commonly believed (and increasingly more common), it is worth drawing students' attention to this matter to prevent 'over-liberal' usage which gives a false impression of personal originality of thought. Unit 3, Task 9, text 6 shows an (arguably less common) abundant use of the first person.

(There is further discussion on the use of the first person on page 33 of this book.)

Task 8: Answers

Point out that a conclusion is not synonymous with a summary, nor does it have to contain one. In the conventions of some academic traditions, the two may be viewed as being the same.

Feature 1. Conclusion 1, first three sentences.
Conclusion 2, first paragraph.
Conclusion 3, whole paragraph (though it is not just a summary).

Feature 2. Conclusion 1, first sentence.
Note that in a *short* essay, a conclusion is very likely to include this. The conclusion at the end of a longer piece of writing, such as the articles here, is likely to recapitulate any deductions that have already been made in the main body.

Feature 3. Conclusion 1, 'An obvious direction …' could be an impersonally expressed personal view (which is later retracted).

Feature 4. More likely to come in an introduction but not to be ruled out in a conclusion, as conclusion 4 shows.

Feature 5. Conclusion 1, last sentence.
Conclusion 2, second paragraph, first sentence.
Conclusion 3, second sentence.

Feature 6. Conclusion 2, third paragraph, last two sentences.
Conclusion 3, fourth sentence, 'While this will reduce …'.
Conclusion 4, first paragraph, second sentence.

Feature 7. Conclusion 2, last paragraph, last three sentences.
Conclusion 4, first paragraph, second paragraph, last sentence.

Feature 8. Unlikely that important *new* information will appear in a conclusion, though there appears to be some in conclusion 4.

TASK 9: ANSWERS

5. Introduction ⟶ 1. Conclusion
2. Introduction ⟶ 7. Conclusion
3. Introduction ⟶ 8. Conclusion
4. Introduction ⟶ 6. Conclusion

TASK 10: ANSWERS

Apart from offering a short 'model' of an academic essay, this section offers a more ambitious set of tasks evaluating introductions and conclusions. The exercise is slightly artificial in that the main body of the essay is short, given the length of the most suitable introduction and conclusion. This has been done to allow the task to be done in class time, if necessary, but at the same time ensuring that as many of the characteristics identified in Tasks 7 and 8 above are included in the correct selections.

The acceptable alternatives are not to be judged *solely* in terms of the features identified in Tasks 7 and 8, though they do contain many of these features (viz. features 1–5 from 'Introductions' in introduction 4 below; features 1, 2, 6 and 7 from 'Conclusions' in conclusion 6 below).

Other criteria (not previously discussed in Unit 3) will have to be taken into consideration in deciding acceptability – namely, factual accuracy, completeness of information, relevance, length and, in two cases, style (introduction 6 and conclusion 3). Some of these criteria have been considered in other contexts in this material (see especially the section on 'Summarising' in Unit 2).

Brief attention to style is also given in Unit 5. The purpose of including some focus on this is, firstly, to provide a challenge for better students and, secondly, to raise students' awareness of other needs to address in their writing. Any attempt at a more exhaustive treatment of matters of style lies outside the scope of this book.

With some groups it may be advisable to start Task 10 by asking students to ascertain a suitable title for the essay. The essay on international migration can be used as a model of the skills of reporting, referencing and writing quotations practised in Unit 3. The fourth bibliography task in Unit 4 (Task 5) is a list of references for this essay.

1.	Introduction	Comment
	1	Incomplete and seriously lacking balance; there is no discussion of Petras's model in the main body.
	2	Inaccurate – the essay does not consider movements only 'in the light of economic considerations'.
	3	Accurate (though, arguably, too repetitive of the content of the main body, given the length of the latter).
	4	The most suitable – accurate and thorough.
	5	Incomplete – gives little idea of the content of the main body. Second paragraph indicates the content of only the 'next part', an occasional fault in students' introductions.
	6	Inadequate – vague opening with unacknowledged quotation, followed by an apparently cynical comment, insubstantial in its link to the main body.

2.	Conclusion	Comment
	1	Inaccurate – stresses the economic too much and recapitulates the theory mentioned in introduction 1 above which is not touched on in the main body. The concluding deduction is not one that can soundly be made on the basis of what is discussed in the main body.
	2	Acceptable; however, the point about concern over immigration levels is not given great attention in the text and not developed in the conclusion.
	3	Completely unsuitable! Getting students to articulate exactly why can be exploited towards a discussion on appropriateness of style and ideas.
	4	Unsatisfactory – vague, sweeping statements and facile observations.
	5	Adequate, even if it is principally a summary. Arguably too long and repetitive of content of main body, considering length of the latter.
	6	Preferable to 2 or 5, though students may argue a lot about which of these three is the most suitable!

TASK 11: ANSWERS

Extract 1 – (d)	Extract 3 – (c)	Extract 5 – (e)
Extract 2 – (b)	Extract 4 – (a)	

It may be worth drawing students' attention to the style of documentation in extracts 1, 4, and 5. In 1 and 4, the numbers in parentheses refer to a list of references; in 5, they are page numbers in the work of the author mentioned. The styles conform to those commonly used in science (1 and 4) and the humanities (5). (Extract 2 is on the philosophy of science – numbers after dates are page numbers. Extract 3 comes from an economics essay.)

UNIT 4 *TOWARDS EXTENDED WRITING*

AIMS

The aim of Unit 4 is for students to produce an extended piece of writing, of 800–1,300 words, in their own subject area. The essay is intended to be an introduction for the non-specialist. Work covered in this unit, together with that in previous units, should provide the necessary skills for students to approach this task successfully. You may like to give a brief review of the skills practised and discussed so far before students attempt the writing task.

It should be emphasised that the writing task at the end of this unit is intended to ensure that students have successfully acquired the skills practised in Units 1–4. Over-absorption in content should be discouraged until Unit 5, except in the case of students who clearly have little trouble with any of the skills.

There are few formal tasks in Unit 4, and even fewer in Unit 5, as by this stage in the material students are expected to have developed their enabling skills and become semi-autonomous in their production of a piece of extended writing.

The Guide for Unit 4 contains the following sections:

1. Tables and figures in an academic paper
2. Layout of written work
3. The stages of extended writing.

Apart from the extended writing task, there are tasks on incorporating tables and illustrations and on compiling a bibliography or list of references at the end of a piece of writing. You should point out to students that variations exist and that they should check on the preferred system in their subject area.

Students often produce bibliographies not even approximating to a correct form because they are unfamiliar with the basics or consider them unimportant. Work on bibliographies in this unit aims to ensure a basic competence: going into greater detail (considering conventions in specific disciplines) has been avoided.

TASK 1: ANSWERS

   (a) Registered full-time students at University of Reading ...
   (b) Road and rail passenger transport use

(c) Air pollution: emissions …
(d) The relative contribution to the greenhouse effect …
(e) Students in further education …
(f) Destination of first degree students

Task 2: Answers

1. (a) book
   (b) (1) joint authors
       (2) title of book
       (3) publisher

2. (a) article in collected edition
   (b) (1) title of article
       (2) names of the editors
       (3) title of the book

3. (a) publication by an institution
   (b) (1) reporting institution
       (2) place of publication
       (3) publisher

4. (a) article in a journal
   (b) (1) title of article
       (2) volume number
       (3) issue number
       (4) page numbers

5. (a) article in a journal
   (b) (1) title of article
       (2) title of journal
       (3) number of volume

Task 3: Answers

The first reference is complete.

DULAY *et al.* lacks name of *place* of publication – Oxford: Oxford University Press. Also, the title should be underlined or italicised.

STERN lacks the publisher's name – Oxford University Press. It should be placed at the end.

RAIMES lacks volume and issue numbers of the periodical and a complete date – vol. 19, no. 2, June.

WHITE lacks a date – (1988).

Task 4: Answers

Bibliographies 1 and 2 are entirely acceptable and the most common forms found across all subjects. However, variations do exist and students should be advised to consult their supervisors when they start their main course to find out whether their subject specialisation/department has any particular conventions. Bibliography 3 is not acceptable under any circumstances.

Task 5: Answers

The correct sequence of titles in alphabetical order is given below. This corresponds to the second bibliography style used in Task 4. (The first bibliography style is more common in the humanities; the one given here tends to be favoured in the social sciences.)

ARNOLD, F. (1990) 'International migration: who goes where?', *Finance and Development*, Vol. 27, No. 2, June, pp. 46–7.

BOHNING, W. R. (1984) *Studies in International Migration*, London: Macmillan.

JACKSON, J. A. (ed.), (1969) *Migration*, Cambridge: Cambridge University Press.

JACOBSON, J. L. (1989) *Environmental Refugees: A yardstick of habitability*, Washington DC: Worldwatch Institute.

MARSHALL, R. (1984) 'Immigration: an international economic perspective', *International Migration Review*, Vol. xviii, No. 3, pp. 593–95.

MELANDER, G. and NOBEL, P. (eds), (1978) *African Refugees and the Law*, Uppsala: Scandinavian Institute of African Studies.

PETRAS, E. (1981) 'The global labour market in the modern world economy', in Kritz, M. M., Keely, C. B. and Tomasi, S. M. (eds), *Global Trends in Migration*, New York: Center for Migration Studies.

SADIK, N. (1990) *The State of the World Population 1990*, New York: UN Population Fund.

WIDGREN, J. (1990) 'International migration and regional stability', *International Affairs*, Vol. 66, No. 4, pp. 749–66.

5 WRITING THE EXTENDED ESSAY

AIMS

The aims of Unit 5 are very similar to those of Unit 4: that is, to produce an extended piece of writing in the student's subject area following academic conventions. However, whereas the task in Unit 4 concentrated on giving a general introduction to a specialist subject area, the task in Unit 5 is more specific.

Hopefully, students will have thought about the content of their Unit 5 essay earlier on in the course so that the guidelines for choosing a topic in the Guide may be redundant here. Students should choose a topic related to their area of study and treat it in depth. The topic chosen could be an aspect of their specialisation introduced in the Unit 4 essay, and examined more closely now. Alternatively, they might choose a totally different topic. The topic chosen should, however, be familiar to the student or of particular relevance to his/her future course of study, if possible. In this way, students will deepen their knowledge of a pertinent subject area, while also developing their critical abilities. Treating a topic in more depth will force students to be more selective when choosing source materials and evaluating their selection carefully.

Unit 4 should have served as a kind of 'dress rehearsal' for the final task. Thus, students will now have the opportunity to improve upon any areas of weakness revealed in their Unit 4 essay.

Suggested procedure

1. Discuss the Guide section. Note that students should introduce the abbreviations into their own work *only* if they are confident as to their exact use.

2. Discuss with your class the main task: – to produce an extended piece of writing of 2,000–3,000 words on a specific area of their subject specialism. For weaker students the task may be shortened and simplified. All students must remember to use their own words when writing and include references to source materials.

3. Discuss any common problems which were revealed in the Unit 4 extended writing task. This may include appropriate semi-specialist vocabulary or areas for remedial grammar treatment. Give help with the features typical of objective academic writing.

4. Draw attention to the importance of revising and proof-reading. Reading aloud can help to find spelling and typographical errors, in the absence of a computer 'spelling check'.

ADDITIONAL TASK: ANSWERS

This is an optional additional task which you should do only if there is enough time and you feel your students will be able to do it with relatively little trouble. It might be worth emphasising to students that they are not expected to consider content (as in some previous tasks with this format) or grammar. The objective of this task is to raise students' awareness of what may be for them less obvious types of error than grammar and spelling. As pointed out in the Student's Book, it is not intended to give anything like an exhaustive survey of the types of fault included. The extract at the beginning presents information in an acceptable way – it shows none of the faults of style, register or word choice in the pieces that follow.

Text 1. Colloquial style; use contracted verbs.

Text 2. A few students might think that this kind of rhetoric can be used to get a point home; in fact, it is not uncommon to find a sequence of questions in academic writing, but not leading up to the kind of answer given here! This paragraph is really included to give students a little confidence in spotting inappropriate style!

Text 3. Verbosity – difficult to tackle particularly in writers whose L1 is a Latin language. There may be students who are convinced that this is an example of good style.

Text 4. Misuse of markers: 'as a matter of fact', 'it can be said that'; 'indeed' used together with 'in fact'.

Text 5. Use of first person singular in stating an opinion – a common fault, often among students who, having been told they have to think for themselves, resort to inappropriate ways of expressing their own views. Point out that the opportunity for giving genuine personal opinion (as opposed to reporting that of an authority or a commonly held opinion) may be relatively rare in the sciences and social sciences, unless one is doing doctoral or post-doctoral work. (See also the brief discussion of this in the notes to Unit 3, Task 7 in this book.) This does not mean that students should avoid the use of the first person in reporting what they have done or found, as in 'we conducted the research' or 'my findings are listed below'. However, they should be careful when expressing *opinion*.

Text 6. Spoken (formal) form. (Note that some students may think that asking a direct question in written English in unacceptable. In fact, it is not uncommon.)

Text 7. Emotive, sweeping statements – 'it is absolute nonsense …', 'only a completely naive simpleton …', 'it is patently obvious'.

Text 8. Cliché – two common ones: 'last but not least' and 'to … or not to …'; 'few and far between' is arguably also one and may inevitably lead to

---

discussion about what expressions are really clichés. Again, as in other parts of this material, making students aware of the fault is important but it is difficult to be prescriptive. They cannot be expected to have the sensitivity to clichés that comes from a native exposure to them.

Text 9. This may be acceptable linguistically in academic writing, but the choice of reporting verbs does not suit what is in the original. Though we do not have access to all of the original text, the cautious attitude adopted by Grant in the extract is wholly inconsistent with the use of 'established conclusively' and 'discovered' here. As stressed in Unit 3, students should be discouraged from using reporting verbs indiscriminately.

APPENDIX 1: SUGGESTED MARKING SCHEME

The following is a revised version of a marking scheme that was used on the CALS Pre-sessional Course at Reading University to assess the extended essays in Units 4 and 5. The band descriptors should be treated as guidelines rather than being rigidly prescriptive. To be placed in a particular band, a student's work need not meet all the criteria assigned to the band.

In assessing content, the problem of teachers being unfamiliar with students' subject matter may arise. It is not always possible to match teachers of English for Academic Purposes with students in a subject area in which the former have some background or interest. Moreover, it is unrealistic to assume the same degree of subject familiarity as the student even if this does happen. This does not preclude the assessment of content with a possible high degree of 'impression-marking'.

The marks given in the right-hand columns are the maximum to be allotted for each band. There is a considerable difference between marks allotted for content in marking the Unit 4 and Unit 5 essays. This is designed to reflect the importance of emphasising non-content features in the students' first extended essay.

	Marks allotted	
	Unit 4	**Unit 5** (MAX.)
Content		
EXCELLENT–VERY GOOD Appears relevant to topic, thorough in coverage and wide in scope.	5	20
GOOD–ADEQUATE Appears relevant but may be a little limited in scope; possibly too detailed in places or too long.	4/3	15
FAIR–INADEQUATE Appears partly irrelevant (despite possible high language proficiency); may be very limited in scope.	2	10
POOR–TOTALLY INADEQUATE Clearly unable to deal with topic competently; may be largely irrelevant or too brief to assess.	1/0	5
Use of source material		
EXCELLENT–VERY GOOD Source material satisfactorily incorporated; quotations used judiciously; complete absence of plagiarism; adequate bibliography.	30	25

GOOD–ADEQUATE Adequate reference to source material though there may be minor errors; absence of plagiarism though possible over-use of quotations; bibliography may be incomplete, or inadequate in minor ways.	22	16
FAIR–INADEQUATE Inadequate reference to source material – quotations incorporated wrongly; some plagiarism in evidence; several types of error in bibliography.	14	10
POOR–TOTALLY INADEQUATE Largely or wholly plagiarised; no quotations or reference to sources; no bibliography or very inadequate one.	7	4

Organisation

EXCELLENT–VERY GOOD Outline of main ideas easily intelligible to reader (even to a non-specialist); sections and paragraphs clearly marked; clear, thorough introduction and conclusion.	15	15
GOOD–ADEQUATE Some incompleteness or lack of clarity in the whole; sections and paragraphs not divided perfectly; introduction and conclusion not perfectly related to main body.	12	12
FAIR–INADEQUATE Outline of main ideas difficult to establish; sections and paragraphs sometimes inadequately divided; introduction and/or conclusion inadequate.	8	8
POOR–TOTALLY INADEQUATE Lack of organisation makes reading very difficult; little or no division into sections and/or paragraphs; poor introduction and/or conclusion or none.	4	4

Cohesion

EXCELLENT–VERY GOOD Close, intelligible relationship between one sentence and another; satisfactory use of connectives.	10	10
GOOD–ADEQUATE Relationship between sentences may occasionally lack smoothness; some misuse of connectives.	7/8	7/8
FAIR–INADEQUATE Unsatisfactory cohesion may make comprehension of parts difficult; many connectives misused or repeated too often.	4/5	4/5
POOR–TOTALLY INADEQUATE Cohesion almost totally absent – writing so fragmentary that comprehension is very difficult; very limited command of connectives.	2	2

Presentation

EXCELLENT–VERY GOOD Clear and legible (if hand-written); includes contents page; correct spacing and/or indentation of paragraphs; any tables or figures well presented.	10	10
GOOD–ADEQUATE May be lacking in one of the above.	7/8	7/8

FAIR–INADEQUATE Presentation makes reading arduous; contents page may be missing; cramped text; tables or figures incomplete or unclear.	4/5	4/5
POOR–TOTALLY INADEQUATE Partly or wholly illegible; may lack margins and contents page; badly spaced.	2	2

Language

EXCELLENT–VERY GOOD Very few language errors.	20	15
GOOD–ADEQUATE Some language errors evident but these rarely impede comprehension.	15	12
FAIR–INADEQUATE Frequent language errors, sometimes impeding comprehension.	10	8
POOR–TOTALLY INADEQUATE Number and type of error make comprehension frequently or totally impossible.	5	4

Mechanical accuracy

EXCELLENT–VERY GOOD Virtually no errors of punctuation, spelling or capitalisation.	10	5
GOOD–ADEQUATE Occasional errors in above but these rarely impede comprehension.	7/8	4/3
FAIR–ADEQUATE Frequent errors in above causing occasional incomprehension.	4/5	2
POOR–TOTALLY INADEQUATE Errors in almost every sentence.	2	1

APPENDIX 2: EXTRA TASK ON NOTE-TAKING

Make photocopies of the text below. Use this extra task at the most suitable stage in Unit 2 where your students will benefit most.

TASK

Read Text A on the following pages and consider how easy it would be to take notes from it. Try taking notes on it yourself, allowing a maximum time limit of five minutes. Then look at the information in Text B and try taking notes on it in the same amount of time.

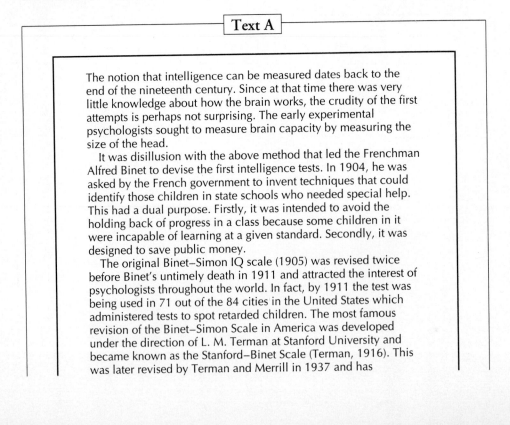

Text A

The notion that intelligence can be measured dates back to the end of the nineteenth century. Since at that time there was very little knowledge about how the brain works, the crudity of the first attempts is perhaps not surprising. The early experimental psychologists sought to measure brain capacity by measuring the size of the head.

It was disillusion with the above method that led the Frenchman Alfred Binet to devise the first intelligence tests. In 1904, he was asked by the French government to invent techniques that could identify those children in state schools who needed special help. This had a dual purpose. Firstly, it was intended to avoid the holding back of progress in a class because some children in it were incapable of learning at a given standard. Secondly, it was designed to save public money.

The original Binet–Simon IQ scale (1905) was revised twice before Binet's untimely death in 1911 and attracted the interest of psychologists throughout the world. In fact, by 1911 the test was being used in 71 out of the 84 cities in the United States which administered tests to spot retarded children. The most famous revision of the Binet–Simon Scale in America was developed under the direction of L. M. Terman at Stanford University and became known as the Stanford–Binet Scale (Terman, 1916). This was later revised by Terman and Merrill in 1937 and has subsequently been updated again (Terman and Merrill, 1937, 1960, 1973).

Besides the Stanford–Binet tests and their revisions, some of the most widely used of modern IQ tests were devised in the United States by David Wechsler. The first version of the Wechsler–Bellevue Intelligence Scale was published in 1939. One of the principal aims in its preparation was to provide an intelligence test suitable for adults rather than schoolchildren, which had been the case of previous work.

Though modern tests based on the approach originally devised by Binet and later modified by others continue to be used, there has for some years been considerable controversy over their validity.

Early proponents of testing often made exaggerated claims about the validity of their results. Some suggested that intelligence was an absolute value like height or weight. Others claimed that it was uniform and unchanging throughout the world.

Criticisms of IQ testings were, in the first instance, undoubtedly a reaction to such extreme positions. However, they have also emerged due to the disturbing potential of test results as a tool of discrimination against groups who have scored less well on average than other groups. This fact has often led to justifiable accusations of cultural bias in test content.

Some recent views of intelligence have suggested that traditional testing may only account for a limited number of abilities. Modern research has revealed the immense complexity of the brain but we know little more about how it works than we did when measuring head size was taken seriously. It may be that, as some clinical psychologists have pointed out, intelligence cannot be viewed separately from personality as a whole.

Dissatisfaction with present methods will no doubt pave the way for new approaches. Wechsler's position on testing IQ reflects the views of modest modern-day proponents. He denied that any absolute value could be given to intelligence. Rather, he hoped that tests could give some indication of an individual's ability to understand and deal with the world. The particular skills, such as quantitative or verbal ability, measured by the component part of his test did not interest him.

Contemporary defence of the use of IQ tests is based on modest claims. Firstly, selection is an inescapable feature of most societies. The need for criteria to help identify less capable students or choose the right job applicant cannot be avoided.

Secondly, some traditional criteria of selection may not be reliable, for example, judging by personal appearance or membership of the right 'old school tie' network.

Thirdly, since they measure a mixture of cognitive skills rather than specific, acquired knowledge, IQ tests may have a higher degree of objectivity. This does not mean that they can be relied on as a sole indicator of ability but that they may have some value in supplementing other criteria.

Text B

Modern IQ tests are largely based on the approach originally devised by Alfred Binet in France and later modified by others or, more recently, the scale pioneered by David Wechsler in the United States. Controversy regarding the validity of testing intelligence has tended to grow in recent years even though the approach is much more sophisticated than the first attempts at the end of the 19th century.

Before Binet was approached by the French government to invent techniques that could identify children requiring special help in state schools, attempts at measuring brain capacity focused on measuring the size of the head. Our knowledge of how the brain works is not much greater today than it was then, though we are more aware of its immense complexity. It may be that, even today, our perception of intelligence is very limited and that testing only accounts for a limited number of abilities. Some clinical psychologists have maintained that intelligence cannot be viewed separately from personality as a whole.

Dissatisfaction with present methods will no doubt pave the way for new approaches just as it did in Binet's case when he became disillusioned with measuring heads. The appearance of the Binet–Simon IQ scale in 1905 was, in addition, propelled by the desire of the French government to save money and avoid holding back the progress of children in a class because some of them were not capable of learning at a given standard.

Binet's test and its subsequent revisions in France and the United States focused on measuring the intelligence of school-children. One of the principal aims of the Wechsler–Bellevue Intelligence Scale, published in 1939, was to provide a test suitable for adults.

Though Wechsler extended the application of tests, he was cautious in his claims. In his view, intelligence could never be measured to give an absolute value in the way that, for example, height and weight can. Moreover, he was not interested in particular skills measured by the component parts of his tests, such as quantitive or verbal ability. He hoped that tests could give some indication of an individual's ability to understand and deal with the world. His modest views reflect the position of more moderate advocates of testing today.

Prior to the Wechsler–Bellevue Scale, there had been several revisions of the Binet–Simon Scale following its founder's untimely death in 1911. By that time, his work had attracted the attention of psychologists throughout the world and was being used in 71 out of the 84 cities in the United States which administered tests to spot retarded children. The most well-known revision of the Binet–Simon Scale in America was developed under the direction of L. M. Terman at Stanford University and became known as the Stanford-Binet Scale (Terman, 1916). Its most recent revision was in 1973, having previously been updated on two occasions (Terman and Merrill, 1937, 1960, 1973).

Some early proponents of testing made exaggerated claims about the validity of their results. It was sometimes claimed that intelligence was an absolute value which was uniform and unchanging throughout the world.

Criticisms of IQ testing were, in the first instance, undoubtedly a reaction to such extreme positions. However, they have also emerged due to the disturbing potential of test results as a tool of discrimination against groups who have scored less well on average than other groups. This fact has frequently led to justifiable accusations of cultural bias in text content.

Modern defence of the use of tests is based on modest claims. It can be argued that selection is an inescapable feature of most societies. The need for criteria to help identify less capable students or choose the right job applicant cannot be avoided. Some traditional criteria of selection, such as judging by appearance or membership of the right 'old school tie' network, may not be as reliable as IQ tests. Since they measure a mixture of cognitive skills rather than specific, acquired knowledge, these tests may have a higher degree of objectivity. This does not mean that they can be relied on as a sole indicator of ability but that they may have some value in supplementing other criteria.

If you tried taking notes on the above two texts, you will have found that it was easier to do so from Text A. Although the content of the two texts is the same, in Text B, it is presented in a non-linear way making it difficult to extricate important information.

A first 'skeleton' of notes on the above texts, identifying functions and some key information might look something like this:

History of measurement of intelligence

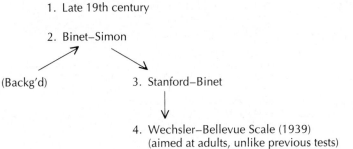

1. Late 19th century

2. Binet–Simon

(Backg'd)

3. Stanford–Binet

4. Wechsler–Bellevue Scale (1939)
(aimed at adults, unlike previous tests)

Arguments for and against IQ testing

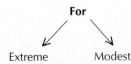

For   Against

Extreme   Modest

Below is a completed set of notes in which information has been added to the 'skeleton'.

History of measurement of intelligence

      1. Late 19th century – meas. size of head

      2. 1st. intel. test Binet–Simon (1905)

          (Backg'd)

Binet – dissat. with 1st method
Asked by Fr. govmt. to dev. tests to
spot children needing special help

    Interest throughout world esp. US
    Revised by Terman

      3. Stanford–Binet Scale (1916)
         Revised by Terman & Merrill
         (1937, 1960, 1973)

Arguments for and against IQ testing

For   **Against**

Extreme
Int. an absolute value;
uniform & unchanging

Modest
1 Not absolute; useful
  as general indicator
  to supplement other
  criteria

2 Higher degree of
  objectivity than
  trad'l other criteria

3 Selection a feature
  of society

1 Tests may account for
  only a few types of
  int.

2 Cultural bias in test
  content

3 Results may be used
  as tool of
  discrimination

We could equally well make use of a 'mind map'. In fact, this may be more useful in sorting out information which is not presented in an easily distinguishable linear form, as in the second example above. Look at the 'mind map' below of information in the above texts.

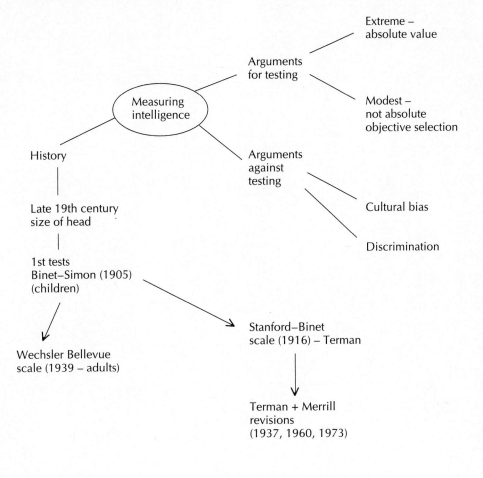